1

Dandelion Book 1, Dictation

Step by Step
Spelling, Dictation and Punctuation for KS1
Complements Dandelion Books
Units 1-20

Contents

Introduction

Who is this workbook for?

English spelling is difficult to learn. In Year Reception, children are taught the first sound/symbol correspondences of the English Phonic Code. Children with a good visual memory and a good grasp of sound/symbol correspondences will make steady progress in spelling. Others may fall behind. This could be due to hearing loss, poor visual memory, immaturity and concentration difficulties or poor sequencing skills. These children will enter Year 1 needing to revise the spelling taught in Reception before taking on the more complex sound/symbol correspondences taught in Year 1. This workbook is aimed at those children.

Why is dictation an effective way of teaching spelling?

Writing is a very complex activity which entails thinking of what to write in a meaningful sequence, using correct spelling and letter formation. Dictation exercises allow the pupil to concentrate on accurate spelling without having to worry about the rest.
Dictation also enables the teacher to provide the practice of a specific spelling focus at the pupil's level. The teacher selects a dictation with a phonic focus that has been taught. Dictation brings about opportunities for practice and success.

Dictation exercises also develop the pupil's ability to revise written work.

What is the spelling progression in this workbook?

The aim of this workbook is for the pupil to experience spelling success at each stage of this workbook. The dictation exercises follow the step-by-step phonic progression of the Dandelion Books reading scheme. Each unit is a new level that introduces new sound/symbol correspondences or spelling skills. These match the same numbered unit in the reading scheme.

How are high-frequency words introduced?

As in the reading scheme, high-frequency words with complex spellings are introduced gradually as they often include difficult spellings beyond the spelling level of the pupil. These words are highlighted within the worksheets. They are not the focus of the exercises and the teacher may choose to ignore them when spelled incorrectly.

How should children be taught to spell?

The most effective way to teach spelling is through a multi-sensory approach which will include seeing, hearing and forming letters. This will help the pupil to internalise and remember the spellings taught. Pupils who need extra support may benefit from additional sensory input such as forming the words using plasticene or drawing them in a sand tray.

What about poor letter formation?

Letter formation and spelling are two separate skills. Some children have difficulty forming their letters correctly. When working on dictation and spelling, it would be preferable to focus on the spelling and to ignore the letter formation unless it is indecipherable. Separate handwriting lessons can offer the pupil practice in correct letter formation.

Where to start?

A diagnostic word spelling test is included to help the teacher identify the correct level for the pupil. The pupil should work through the diagnostic spelling list. The first incorrect spelling will indicate the spelling level of the pupil. It is recommended to start a level or two lower in order to build the pupil's confidence and skills.

Reading and spelling single words

The first reading and spelling sheet introduces single words. This sheet reinforces blending and segmenting, the underlying skills of reading and spelling and connects them one to the other. The pupil reads the words. Then he/she is dictated the same words. Lines within each word direct the pupil to place the letter spelling each sound in the correct place.

If the pupil has difficulty with this activity, the teacher will need to support him/her through word-building exercises. The teacher can use plastic or wooden letters to build the words in the workbook. The pupil should then practice writing the word (preferably on a whiteboard) saying the sounds as he/she spells the word.

Reading and spelling sentences

This dictation exercise extends the pupil to segmenting words within whole sentences. The pupil is required to copy the text in the scroll and segment the words on the lines below. High-frequency words with complex spellings are spelled for the pupil. These sheets can also be dictated to the pupil, by folding and hiding the scroll from the pupil. After the dictation, the pupil can self-correct his/her work.

How to dictate a word or sentence

It is important to dictate words and sentences in a way that allows the pupil to hear, comprehend and retain the word or sentence dictated. When dictating a word, say the word, then say a sentence with the word in it (so that the pupil understands the word) and then repeat the word again. This should be done at the pace the pupil is comfortable with. When dictating a sentence, say it once and repeat it. If the sentence is too long for the pupil to remember, break it up into parts, pausing for the pupil to write the words in each phrase at a comfortable pace.

Punctuation exercises

Many children have difficulty punctuating their written work. This workbook offers step-by-step introduction to the following concepts and skills:

1. Understanding that a sentence starts with a capital letter and ends with a full stop.
2. Identifying where a sentence ends.
3. Indentifying where a sentence begins.
4. Indentifying the sentences and adding full stops and capital letters - with support.
5. Finding the sentences and adding the capital letters and full stops independently.

		✓		✓		✓		✓		✓		Notes
Lesson 1	sit		mat									
Lesson 2	pat		not									
Lesson 3	big		cat		hop							
Lesson 4	fan		vet		bed							
Lesson 5	kid		run		lad							
Lesson 6	jet		win		zip							
Lesson 7	box		yes		doll		mess		fizz			
Lesson 8	jump		sand		rest		and					
Lesson 9	grab		stop		bless		trap					
Lesson 10	plums		slept		crisp		strict					
Lesson 11	chest		lunch									
Lesson 12	shop		fish									
Lesson 13	thin		that		broth							
Lesson 14	black		socks		check							
Lesson 15	song		swing		fling							
Lesson 16	quest		have		quick		gives					
Lesson 17	when		which		upset		cannot					
Lesson 18	blinked		landed		dragged							
Lesson 19	blocking		wishing		singing							
Lesson 20	apple		bottle		middle		stumbles					

Dandelion Book of Dictation

This book belongs to

Lesson 1 – Unit 1

Dictation

Make sure pupils recognise the sounds these letters represent and can form them correctly:

s, a, t, i, m

Read each sentence twice before the learner writes it down. If necessary, write the high-frequency with complex spellings (which have been highlighted) on a board for the learner to refer to.

Tam sat.
Sit, Tim.
Sam sat.
Is it Sam?
I am Tam.
Sam sat **on the** mat.

High-frequency words with complex spellings in the above text are:

is, I, on, the

Lesson 1 - Unit 1: s, a, t, i, m

Reading and spelling VC, CVC words

am	✓	___ ___	
at		___ ___	
it		___ ___	
sat		___ ___ ___	
sit		___ ___ ___	
mat		___ ___ ___	
Sam		___ ___ ___	
Tam		___ ___ ___	
Tim		___ ___ ___	

Teaching aims: Reading and spelling VC, CVC words

Teaching guidelines: Fold this sheet along the dotted line. Ask the pupil to read the words on the left and tick the words she/he has read correctly. Ask the pupil to turn over the sheet and dictate the words to the pupil. Ask the pupil to spell the words by segmenting and sounding out the sounds as she/he writes them on the lines. Ask the pupil to open the sheet and tick the words she/he has spelled correctly.

Reading and spelling

Is it Sam?

I am Tam.

Tim sat on the mat.

Is __ __ __ __ __?

I __ __ __ __ __.

__ __ __ __ __ __ on the __ __ __.

Copy the text in the top scroll to the bottom scroll. Write a sound on each line e.g.: m a t. This activity can also be used for dictation. Fold the sheet over. The pupil can self-correct his/her own dictation. This sheet may be photocopied by the purchaser. © Phonic Books Ltd 2013.

Lesson 1 - Unit 1

Punctuation - capital letters and full stops

REMINDER – A sentence **starts** with a capital letter and **ends** with a full stop.

Tam sat.	__am sat
Sit, Tim.	__it, Tim
Tam sat on the mat.	__am sat on the mat
It is Sam.	__t is Sam
Sam is on the mat.	__am is on the mat
It is Tim.	__t is Tim
Tim sat on the mat.	__im sat on the mat

Ask the pupil to read the sentence on the right and then correct the sentence on the left by putting in the capital letter and full stop. This sheet may be photocopied by the purchaser.
© Phonic Books Ltd 2013.

Lesson 2 – Unit 2

Dictation

Make sure pupils recognise the sounds these letters represent and can form them correctly:

n, o, p

Read each sentence twice before the learner writes it down. If necessary, write the high-frequency words with complex spellings (which have been highlighted) on a board for the learner to refer to.

Pip **is** on **a** mop.
A man sat on **a** mat.
A tin **is** on **the** mat.
Pam **is** in **the** pot.

High-frequency words with complex spellings in the above text are:

is, a, the

Lesson 2 - Unit 2: n, o, p

Reading and spelling VC and CVC words

an	✓	___ ___	
in		___ ___	
on		___ ___	
pin		___ ___ ___	
nap		___ ___ ___	
tin		___ ___ ___	
tap		___ ___ ___	
top		___ ___ ___	
tip		___ ___ ___	

Teaching aims: Reading and spelling VC and CVC words

Teaching guidelines: Fold this sheet along the dotted line. Ask the pupil to read the words on the left and tick the words she/he has read correctly. Ask the pupil to turn over the sheet and dictate the words to the pupil. Ask the pupil to spell the words by segmenting and sounding out the sounds as she/he writes them on the lines. Ask the pupil to open the sheet and tick the words she/he has spelled correctly.

Reading and spelling

Pip is on a mop.

Pam is in the pot.

Sam is not on the mat.

_ _ _ _ is on a _ _ _.

_ _ _ is _ _ the _ _ _.

_ _ _ is _ _ _ on the _ _ _.

Copy the text in the top scroll to the bottom scroll. Write a sound on each line e.g.: m a t.
This activity can also be used for dictation. Fold the sheet over. The pupil can self-correct
his/her own dictation.   This sheet may be photocopied by the purchaser. © Phonic Books Ltd
2013.

Punctuation - capital letters and full stops

REMINDER – A sentence **starts** with a capital letter and **ends** with a full stop.

Pip is on the mop.	___ip is on the mop
Tim sat on the mat.	___im sat on the mat
A pin is on the top.	___ pin is on the top
The tap is on.	___he tap is on
The mop is on the mat.	___he mop is on the mat
Pam is on Pip.	___am is on Pip
The top is on the mat.	___he top is on the mat

Ask the pupil to read the sentence on the right and then correct the sentence on the left by putting in the capital letter and full stop. This sheet may be photocopied by the purchaser.
© Phonic Books Ltd 2013.

Lesson 3 – Unit 3

Dictation

Make sure pupils recognise the sounds these letters represent and can form them correctly:

b, c, g, h

Read each sentence twice before the learner writes it down. If necessary, write the high-frequency words with complex spellings on a board for the learner to refer to.

Pam sat in **a** big cot.
Cat **is** not in **the** cot.
Pam **has a** big sob.
Pip got **the** cat.
Pip **has his** cap on.

High-frequency words with complex spellings in the above text are:

a, is, the, has, his

16

Lesson 3 - Unit 3: b, c, g, h

Reading and spelling CVC words

cat	✓	___ ___ ___	
bag		___ ___ ___	
hat		___ ___ ___	
sob		___ ___ ___	
got		___ ___ ___	
pig		___ ___ ___	
cab		___ ___ ___	
hot		___ ___ ___	
big		___ ___ ___	

Teaching aims: Reading and spelling CVC words

Teaching guidelines: Fold this sheet along the dotted line. Ask the pupil to read the words on the left and tick the words she/he has read correctly. Ask the pupil to turn over the sheet and dictate the words to the pupil. Ask the pupil to spell the words by segmenting and sounding out the sounds as she/he writes them on the lines. Ask the pupil to open the sheet and tick the words she/he has spelled correctly.

This sheet may be photocopied by the purchaser. © Phonic Books Ltd 2013.

Reading and spelling

Pam had a big sob.

"Cat is not in the cot!"

Pip got the cat.

Pam has the cat.

Pam __ __ __ a __ __ __ __ __ __ __.

"__ __ __ is __ __ __ __ in the __ __ __!"

__ __ __ __ __ __ __ the __ __ __.

__ __ __ __ has the __ __ __.

Copy the text in the top scroll to the bottom scroll. Write a sound on each line e.g.: b i g. This activity can also be used for dictation. Fold the sheet over. The pupil can self-correct his/her own dictation. This sheet may be photocopied by the purchaser. © Phonic Books Ltd 2013.

Lesson 3 – Unit 3

Punctuation - capital letters and full stops

REMINDER – A sentence **starts** with a capital letter and **ends** with a full stop.

Pip has a cap on.	__ip has a cap on
Cat is not in the cot.	__at is not in the cot
A hat is on the mat.	__ hat is on the mat
Pip has got a pan.	__ip has got a pan
The pan is big.	__he pan is big
Bob is a cat.	__ob is a cat
A can is in the bin.	__ can is in the bin

Ask the pupil to read the sentence on the right and then correct the sentence on the left by putting in the capital letter and full stop. This sheet may be photocopied by the purchaser.

Lesson 4 – Unit 4

Dictation

Make sure pupils recognise the sounds these letters represent and can form them correctly:

d, e, f, v

Read each sentence twice before the learner writes it down. If necessary, write the high-frequency words with complex spellings on a board for the learner to refer to.

Bob got **the** cod in **the** bin.
Dan had **a** big, fat pen.
Viv hid **the** big, fat pen.
Ted **is** on **the** bed.
Meg **is** on **the** bed at **the** vet.

High-frequency words with complex spellings in the above text are:

the, a, is

Lesson 4 - Unit 4: d, e, f, v

Reading and spelling CVC words

fed	✓	__ __ __	
vet		__ __ __	
dad		__ __ __	
fan		__ __ __	
had		__ __ __	
fit		__ __ __	
bed		__ __ __	
van		__ __ __	
sad		__ __ __	

Teaching aims: Reading and spelling CVC words

Teaching guidelines: Fold this sheet along the dotted line. Ask the pupil to read the words on the left and tick the words she/he has read correctly. Ask the pupil to turn over the sheet and dictate the words to the pupil. Ask the pupil to spell the words by segmenting and sounding out the sounds as she/he writes them on the lines. Ask the pupil to open the sheet and tick the words she/he has spelled correctly.

Reading and spelling

Dan had a big pen.

Viv got the fat pen.

Meg got on the bed.

___ ___ a ___

___.

___ ___ the ___

___.

___ ___ on the ___.

Copy the text in the top scroll to the bottom scroll. Write a sound on each line e.g.: p e n
This activity can also be used for dictation. Fold the sheet over. The pupil can self-correct
his/her own dictation. This sheet may be photocopied by the purchaser. © Phonic Books Ltd
2013.

Lesson 4 – Unit 4

Punctuation - capital letters and full stops

REMINDER – A sentence **starts** with a capital letter and **ends** with a full stop.

Dan had a big, fat pen.
Viv got the fat pen.
Viv hid the big pen.
Meg has the pen.
It is bad to fib.
A van hit Meg.
The vet set the hip.

__an had a big, fat pen
__iv got the fat pen
__iv hid the big pen
__eg has the pen
__t is bad to fib
__ van hit Meg
__he vet set the hip

Ask the pupil to read the sentence on the right and then correct the sentence on the left by putting in the capital letter and full stop. This sheet may be photocopied by the purchaser.

Lesson 5 – Unit 5

Dictation

Make sure pupils recognise the sounds these letters represent and can form them correctly:

k, l, r, u

Read each sentence twice before the learner writes it down. If necessary, write the high-frequency words with complex spellings on a board for the learner to refer to.

A bus **is** in **the** mud.
The kid **has** got mud in **a** mug.
Ken, **the** rat, sat in **the** sun.
Pip **has** gum on **his** lip.
The lad got Kim in **a** cup.

High-frequency words with complex spellings in the above text are:

a, is, the, has, his

Lesson 5 - Unit 5: k, l, r, u

Reading and spelling VC, CVC words

up	✓	__ __	
bug		__ __ __	
log		__ __ __	
run		__ __	
kid		__ __ __	
let		__ __ __	
rob		__ __ __	
kip		__ __ __	
mud		__ __ __	

Teaching aims: Reading and spelling VC and CVC words

Teaching guidelines: Fold this sheet along the dotted line. Ask the pupil to read the words on the left and tick the words she/he has read correctly. Ask the pupil to turn over the sheet and dictate the words to the pupil. Ask the pupil to spell the words by segmenting and sounding out the sounds as she/he writes them on the lines. Ask the pupil to open the sheet and tick the words she/he has spelled correctly.

Reading and spelling

Ken sat in the sun.

Ken hid in a log.

Bob ran but did not get Ken.

__ __ __   __ __ __   in the __ __ __.

__ __ __   __ __ __   __ __   a __ __ __.

__ __ __   __ __ __   __ __ __

__ __ __   __ __ __   __ __ __

__ __ __.

Copy the text in the top scroll to the bottom scroll. Write a sound on each line e.g.: <u>K e n</u>
This activity can also be used for dictation. Fold the sheet over. The pupil can self-correct
his/her own dictation. This sheet may be photocopied by the purchaser. © Phonic Books Ltd
2013.

Lesson 5 – Unit 5

Punctuation - sentences and full stops

<u>Tasks:</u> Text 1: Read the text and note where the sentences end.

Text 2: Fold the sheet along the dotted lines. Draw the slashes at the end of each sentence. Check your work.

Text 3: Fold the sheet again along the dotted lines. Find the sentences. Put in the full stops with a coloured pencil. Check your work.

1

Pip and Kim sit on a log./ The sun is up./ It is fun./

A lad has a big bun./ Kim and Pip get on the bun./

2

Pip and Kim sit on a log. The sun is up. It is fun.

A lad has a big bun. Kim and Pip get on the bun.

3

Pip and Kim sit on a log The sun is up It is fun

A lad has a big bun Kim and Pip get on the bun

Did you spot 5 full stops?

This exercise is to allow the learners to see the sentence as a unit of meaning. They will need a lot of help with this task initially. Self-correcting their own work will help them understand the task. This sheet may be photocopied by the purchaser. © Phonic Books Ltd 2013.

Lesson 6 – Unit 6

Dictation

Make sure pupils recognise the sounds these letters represent and can form them correctly:

j, w, z

Read each sentence twice before the learner writes it down. If necessary, write the high-frequency words with complex spellings on a board for the learner to refer to.

Liz **has** not got **a** wig.
Ken, **the** rat, did not get wet in **the** log.
Jim ran **to** get **the** jam.
Viv ran but Viv did not win.
The red top had a big zip.

High-frequency words with complex spellings in the above text are:

has, a, the, to

28

Lesson 6 - Unit 6: j, w, z

Reading and spelling CVC words

job	✓	___ ___ ___	
win		___ ___ ___	
zip		___ ___ ___	
jam		___ ___ ___	
wet		___ ___ ___	
zap		___ ___ ___	
jet		___ ___ ___	
wig		___ ___ ___	
jab		___ ___ ___	

Teaching aims: Reading and spelling CVC words

Teaching guidelines: Fold this sheet along the dotted line. Ask the pupil to read the words on the left and tick the words she/he has read correctly. Ask the pupil to turn over the sheet and dictate the words to the pupil. Ask the pupil to spell the words by segmenting and sounding out the sounds as she/he writes them on the lines. Ask the pupil to open the sheet and tick the words she/he has spelled correctly.

Reading and spelling

It was wet.

Ken had to zip his mac up.

Ken ran to jog in the wet mud.

___ ___ was ___ ___ ___.

___ ___ ___ ___ ___ ___ to ___ ___ ___ his

___ ___ ___ ___ ___.

___ ___ ___ ___ ___ ___ to ___ ___ ___ ___ ___

the ___ ___ ___ ___ ___ ___.

Copy the text in the top scroll to the bottom scroll. Write a sound on each line e.g.: w e t
This activity can also be used for dictation. Fold the sheet over. The pupil can self-correct
his/her own dictation. This sheet may be photocopied by the purchaser. © Phonic Books Ltd
2013.

Lesson 6 – Unit 6

Punctuation - sentences and full stops

Tasks: Text 1: Read the text and note where the sentences end.

Text 2: Fold the sheet along the dotted lines. Draw the slashes at the end of end of each sentence. Check your work.

Text 3: Fold the sheet again along the dotted lines. Find the sentences. Put in the full stops with a coloured pencil. Check your work.

1

Jim was in his web./ Jim ran to get jam./ The jam was on his leg./ Jim was sad./ Jim got in to a tub./

2

Jim was in his web. Jim ran to get jam. The jam was on his leg. Jim was sad. Jim got in to a tub.

3

Jim was in his web Jim ran to get jam The jam was on his leg Jim was sad Jim got in to a tub

---

Did you spot 5 full stops?

This exercise is to allow the learners to see the sentence as a unit of meaning. They will need a lot of help with this task initially. Self-correcting their own work will help them understand the task. This sheet may be photocopied by the purchaser. © Phonic Books Ltd 2013.

Lesson 7 – Unit 7

Dictation

Make sure pupils recognise the sounds these letters represent and can form them correctly:

x, y, ff, ll, ss, zz

Read each sentence twice before the learner writes it down. If necessary, write the high-frequency words with complex spellings on a board for the learner to refer to.

Sam **has a** fox in **a** box.

"Yes, **I** will sell **the** doll."

A leg fell off Jill, **the** doll, but Zig will fix it.

Tam will miss **the** bus.

The can **of** pop **has** fizz in it.

The top **for** Zig **has a** red cuff.

High-frequency words with complex spellings in the above text are:

has, a, I, the, of, for

Lesson 7 - Unit 7: x, y, ff, ll, ss, zz

Reading and spelling CVC words

well	✓	—— —— ——	
fuss		—— —— ——	
buzz		—— —— ——	
yes		—— —— ——	
box		—— —— ——	
puff		—— —— ——	
miss		—— —— ——	
mix		—— —— ——	
yell		—— —— ——	

Teaching aims: Reading and spelling CVC words

Teaching guidelines: Fold this sheet along the dotted line. Ask the pupil to read the words on the left and tick the words she/he has read correctly. Ask the pupil to turn over the sheet and dictate the words to the pupil. Ask the pupil to spell the words by segmenting and sounding out the sounds as she/he writes them on the lines. Ask the pupil to open the sheet and tick the words she/he has spelled correctly.

Reading and spelling

Rex is the boss. He can yell.

Jill hid in a box.

Rex is sad. Rex has no pal.

___ __ __ is the __ __ ___.

He __ __ __ __ __ ___.

__ __ __ __ — __ __ __ — __ __ a

__ __ —.

__ __ __ is __ __ __. He __ __ __ no

__ __ —.

Copy the text in the top scroll to the bottom scroll. Write a sound on each line e.g.: R e x
This activity can also be used for dictation. Fold the sheet over. The pupil can self-correct
his/her own dictation.   This sheet may be photocopied by the purchaser. © Phonic Books Ltd
2013.

Lesson 7: Punctuation

Sentences and full stops

<u>Tasks:</u>   Text 1: Read the text and note where the sentences end.

Text 2: Fold the sheet along the dotted lines. Draw the slashes at the end of end of each sentence. Check your work.

Text 3: Fold the sheet again along the dotted lines. Find the sentences. Put in the full stops with a coloured pencil. Check your work.

1

Bob is on the sill./ It is wet./ Bob can not get in./

Jill let Bob in./ Bob got on the bed./ It is a mess./

2

Bob is on the sill. It is wet. Bob can not get in.

Jill let Bob in. Bob got on the bed. It is a mess.

3

Bob is on the sill It is wet Bob can not get in

Jill let Bob in Bob got on the bed It is a mess

Did you spot 6 full stops?

Lesson 8 – Unit 8

Dictation

Words with the following letter pattern:

CVCC
(consonant vowel consonant consonant)

Read each sentence twice before the learner writes it down. If necessary, write the high-frequency words with complex spellings on a board for the learner to refer to.

Bob and Meg jump on **the** bed.

Alf felt **the** gift in **his** hand.

Alf met Hank at **the** camp.

Mum and Sam went on **a** hunt **for the** lost dog.

Pip and Tess sat on **the** soft sand and had **a** rest.

High-frequency words with complex spellings in the above text are:

the, his, a, for

Lesson 8 - Unit 8: CVCC

Reading and spelling CVCC words

Word	✓	Spelling	
jump	✓	— — — —	
gift		— — — —	
land		— — — —	
cost		— — — —	
hunt		— — — —	
help		— — — —	
hand		— — — —	
camp		— — — —	
milk		— — — —	

Teaching aims: Reading and spelling CVCC words

Teaching guidelines: Fold this sheet along the dotted line. Ask the pupil to read the words on the left and tick the words she/he has read correctly. Ask the pupil to turn over the sheet and dictate the words to the pupil. Ask the pupil to spell the words by segmenting and sounding out the sounds as she/he writes them on the lines. Ask the pupil to open the sheet and tick the words she/he has spelled correctly.

Reading and spelling

Alf has an old tent.

Alf met Hank at the dump.

Hank can mend the old tent.

___ ___ ___ has ___ ___   ___ ___ ___

___ ___ ___ ___.

___ ___ ___   ___ ___ ___   ___ ___ ___ ___

___ ___ the ___ ___ ___ ___.

___ ___ ___ ___   ___ ___ ___   ___ ___ ___ ___

The old ___ ___ ___ ___.

Copy the text in the top scroll to the bottom scroll. Write a sound on each line e.g.: <u>A</u> <u>l</u> <u>f</u>
This activity can also be used for dictation. Fold the sheet over. The pupil can self-correct
his/her own dictation. This sheet may be photocopied by the purchaser. © Phonic Books Ltd.
2013.

Lesson 8 – Unit 8

Punctuation - sentences and full stops

Tasks: Text 1: Read the text and note where the sentences end.

Text 2: Fold the sheet along the dotted lines. Draw the slashes at the end of each sentence. Check your work.

Text 3: Fold the sheet again along the dotted lines. Find the sentences. Put in the full stops with a coloured pencil. Check your work.

1

Bob and Meg jump on the bunk bed./ Bob jumps off./ Meg will not jump off./ Viv can help./ Viv lifts Meg off the bed./

2

Bob and Meg jump on the bunk bed. Bob jumps off. Meg will not jump off. Viv can help. Viv lifts Meg off the bed.

3

Bob and Meg jump on the bunk bed Bob jumps off Meg will not jump off Viv can help Viv lifts Meg off the bed

Did you spot 5 full stops?

This exercise is to allow the learners to see the sentence as a unit of meaning. They will need a lot of help with this task initially. Self-correcting their own work will help them understand the task. This sheet may be photocopied by the purchaser. © Phonic Books Ltd 2013.

Lesson 9 – Unit 9

Dictation

Words with the following letter pattern:

CCVC
(consonant consonant vowel consonant)

Read each sentence twice before the learner writes it down. If necessary, write the high-frequency words with complex spellings on a board for the learner to refer to.

Viv must not spill **the** milk.

Mum **is** cross. **The** milk **is** on **the** rug.

Gran pats Floss, **the** dog.

Rex runs **to** grab **the** pram.

A man set **a** trap **for** Flip and Flop.

High-frequency words with complex spellings in the above text are:

the, is, to, for, a

Lesson 9 - Unit 9: CCVC

Reading and spelling CCVC words

grab	✓	— — — —	
flag		— — — —	
plum		— — — —	
stop		— — — —	
twig		— — — —	
drag		— — — —	
swim		— — — —	
stem		— — — —	
trip		— — — —	

Teaching aims: Reading and spelling CCVC words

Teaching guidelines: Fold this sheet along the dotted line. Ask the pupil to read the words on the left and tick the words she/he has read correctly. Ask the pupil to turn over the sheet and dictate the words to the pupil. Ask the pupil to spell the words by segmenting and sounding out the sounds as she/he writes them on the lines. Ask the pupil to open the sheet and tick the words she/he has spelled correctly.

Reading and spelling

Viv and Fred trip and spill the milk.

Mum is cross.

Meg, the dog, laps up the milk.

Viv and Fred are glad.

___ ___ ___ and ___ ___ ___ ___ ___ ___ ___ ___

___ ___ ___ ___ ___ ___ the

___ ___ ___ ___.

___ ___ ___ is ___ ___ ___ ___.

___ ___ ___, the ___ ___ ___, ___ ___ ___ ___

___ ___ the ___ ___ ___ ___.

___ ___ ___ ___ ___ ___ ___ ___ ___

are ___ ___ ___ ___.

Copy the text in the top scroll to the bottom scroll. Write a sound on each line e.g.: t r i p
This activity can also be used for dictation. Fold the sheet over. The pupil can self-correct
his/her own dictation.   This sheet may be photocopied by the purchaser. © Phonic Books Ltd
2013.

Sentences begin with a capital letter

<u>Tasks:</u>   Text 1: Read the text and note where the sentences begin: ☺

Text 2: Fold the sheet along the dotted lines. Draw ☺ at the beginning of each sentence. Check your work.

Text 3: Fold the sheet again along the dotted lines. Find the sentences. Put in the capital letters with a coloured pencil at the beginning of each sentence. Check your work.

1

☺ Jill runs with the pram. ☺ Ted is in the pram. ☺ Jill trips and lets go of the pram. ☺ The pram bumps on the steps. ☺ Rex runs to grab the pram.

2

Jill runs with the pram. Ted is in the pram. Jill trips and lets go of the pram. The pram bumps on the steps. Rex runs to grab the pram.

3

jill runs with the pram. ted is in the pram. jill trips and lets go of the pram. the pram bumps on the steps. rex runs to grab the pram.

Did you spot 5 missing capitals letters?

This exercise is to allow the learners to see the sentence as a unit of meaning. They will need a lot of help with this task initially. Self-correcting their own work will help them understand the task. This sheet may be photocopied by the purchaser. © Phonic Books Ltd 2013.

Lesson 10 – Unit 10

Dictation

Words with the following letter pattern:

CCVCC
(consonant consonant vowel consonant consonant)

Read each sentence twice before the learner writes it down. If necessary, write the high-frequency words with complex spellings on a board for the learner to refer to.

Viv bumps in **to a** box **of** plums.

Alf slept in **a** tent.

Frank swims and rests in **the** pond.

Ken jumps and skips **to** get fit.

Dan trips on **his** stilts and lands in **the** mud.

High-frequency words with complex spellings in the above text are:

to, a, of, the, his

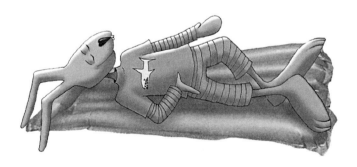

Lesson 10 - Unit 10: CCVCC

Reading and spelling CCVCC words

stand	✓	— — — — — —
crisp		— — — — — —
swims		— — — — — —
stamp		— — — — — —
plums		— — — — — —
spilt		— — — — — —
print		— — — — — —
frogs		— — — — — —
stump		— — — — — —

Teaching aims: Reading and spelling CCVCC words

Teaching guidelines: Fold this sheet along the dotted line. Ask the pupil to read the words on the left and tick the words she/he has read correctly. Ask the pupil to turn over the sheet and dictate the words to the pupil. Ask the pupil to spell the words by segmenting and sounding out the sounds as she/he writes them on the lines. Ask the pupil to open the sheet and tick the words she/he has spelled correctly.

Reading and spelling

Mum is strict.

Viv can not have crisps.

Viv is cross.

Viv stamps and flaps her hands.

__ __ __ is __ __ __ __ __ __.

__ __ __ can not have __ __ __ __ __ __.

__ __ __ is __ __ __ __.

__ __ __ __ __ __ __ __ __ __ __

__ __ __ __ __ her __ __ __ __ __.

Copy the text in the top scroll to the bottom scroll. Write a sound on each line e.g.: f l a p s
This activity can also be used for dictation. Fold the sheet The pupil can self- own dictation.
This sheet may be photocopied by the purchaser. © Phonic Books Ltd 2013.

Sentences and capital letters

<u>Tasks:</u>   Text 1: Read the text and note where the sentences begin: ☺

Text 2: Fold the sheet along the dotted lines. Draw ☺ at the beginning of each sentence. Check your work.

Text 3: Fold the sheet again along the dotted lines. Find the sentences. Put in the capital letters with a coloured pencil at the beginning of each sentence. Check your work.

1

☺ Ken is not fit. ☺ He pants as he runs. ☺ He jumps and skips. ☺ He swims in the pond. ☺ He lifts twigs. ☺ Bob, the cat, can not get him.

2

Ken is not fit. He pants as he runs. He jumps and skips. He swims in the pond. He lifts twigs. Bob, the cat, can not get him.

3

ken is not fit. he pants as he runs. he jumps and skips. he swims in the pond. he lifts twigs. bob, the cat, can not get him.

Did you spot 6 missing capitals letters?

This exercise is to allow the learners to see the sentence as a unit of meaning. They will need a lot of help with this task initially. Self-correcting their own work will help them understand the task. This sheet may be photocopied by the purchaser. © Phonic Books Ltd 2013.

Lesson 11 – Unit 11

Dictation

Words with the following letter pattern:

ch

Read each sentence twice before the learner writes it down. If necessary, write the high-frequency words with complex spellings on a board for the learner to refer to.

Chen and Liz went **to** get chips **for** lunch.
Dad naps on **the** bench.
"Get **to** bed and **no** chit chat," **says** Dad.
Chimp runs and sits on **a** branch.
Stan **has** nuts in **a** chest.

High-frequency words with complex spellings in the above text are:

to, for, the, no, says, a, has

48

Lesson 11 - Unit 11: ch

Reading and spelling words with <ch>

chat	✓	___ ___ ___
chips		___ ___ ___ ___
much		___ ___ ___
chop		___ ___ ___
chill		___ ___ ___
bench		___ ___ ___ ___
chimp		___ ___ ___ ___
chap		___ ___ ___
chest		___ ___ ___

Teaching aims: Reading and spelling words with the <ch> spelling

Teaching guidelines: Fold this sheet along the dotted line. Ask the pupil to read the words on the left and tick the words she/he has read correctly. Ask the pupil to turn over the sheet and dictate the words to the pupil. Ask the pupil to spell the words by segmenting and sounding out the sounds as she/he writes them on the lines. Ask the pupil to open the sheet and tick the words she/he has spelled correctly.

Reading and spelling

Stan's chest is next to a bench.

He has a nut for lunch.

His chums have nuts as well.

_ _ _ _ ' _   _ _ _ _ _ is

_ _ _ _ _ to a _ _ _ _ _ .

He has a _ _ _ for _ _ _ _ .

His _ _ _ _ _ have _ _ _ _ _ as

_ _ _ .

Copy the text in the top scroll to the bottom scroll. Write a sound on each line e.g.: <u>ch</u> <u>e</u> <u>s</u> <u>t</u>
This activity can also be used for dictation. Fold the sheet over. The pupil can self-correct
his/her own dictation.   This sheet may be photocopied by the purchaser. © Phonic Books Ltd
2013.

Sentences and capital letters

<u>Tasks:</u>   Text 1: Read the text and note where the sentences begin: ☺

Text 2: Fold the sheet along the dotted lines. Draw ☺ at the beginning of each sentence. Check your work.

Text 3: Fold the sheet again along the dotted lines. Find the sentences. Put in the capital letters with a coloured pencil at the beginning of each sentence. Check your work.

1

☺ Jill is a champ. ☺ Jill can skip. ☺ Rex is a champ. ☺ Rex can jump. ☺ Chimp is a champ. ☺ Chimp can jump from branch to branch.

2

Jill is a champ. Jill can skip. Rex is a champ. Rex can jump. Chimp is a champ. Chimp can jump from branch to branch.

3

jill is a champ. jill can skip. rex is a champ. rex can jump. chimp is a champ. chimp can jump from branch to branch.

Did you spot 6 missing capitals letters?

This exercise is to allow the learners to see the sentence as a unit of meaning. They will need a lot of help with this task initially. Self-correcting their own work will help them understand the task. This sheet may be photocopied by the purchaser. © Phonic Books Ltd 2013.

Lesson 12 – Unit 12

Dictation

Words with the following letter pattern:

sh

Read each sentence twice before the learner writes it down. If necessary, write the high-frequency words with complex spellings on a board for the learner to refer to.

Shep and Tosh wish **for a** pal.
Shep ran and hid in **a** shrub.
Josh sets up **a** shop.
Dad **is** in **a** fresh fish shop.
The fish **is** on **a** dish.

High-frequency words with complex spellings in the above text are:

for, a, is, the

Lesson 12 - Unit 12: sh

Reading and spelling words with <sh>

shop	✓	—— —— ——
ship		—— — —— ——
dish		—— — —— ——
shall		—— — —— ——
fish		—— — —— ——
crash		—— — —— —— ——
brush		—— — —— ——
shrub		—— — —— ——
plush		—— — —— ——

Teaching aims: Reading and spelling words with the <sh> spelling

Teaching guidelines: Fold this sheet along the dotted line. Ask the pupil to read the words on the left and tick the words she/he has read correctly. Ask the pupil to turn over the sheet and dictate the words to the pupil. Ask the pupil to spell the words by segmenting and sounding out the sounds as she/he writes them on the lines. Ask the pupil to open the sheet and tick the words she/he has spelled correctly.

Reading and spelling

Josh sets up a shop.

Mum asks Josh for the dish for the buns.

Josh sells buns for cash.

__ __ __ __   __ __ __ __   __ __ a

__ __ __ .

__ __ __ __   __ __ __ __ __   __ __ __ __ for

the __ __ __ __ for the __ __ __ __ .

__ __ __ __   __ __ __ __   __ __ __ __

for __ __ __ .

Copy the text in the top scroll to the bottom scroll. Write a sound on each line e.g.: sh o p
This activity can also be used for dictation. Fold the sheet over. The pupil can self-correct
his/her own dictation.   This sheet may be photocopied by the purchaser. © Phonic Books Ltd
2013.

Lesson 12 – Unit 12

Sentences and capital letters

<u>Tasks:</u>   Text 1: Read the text and note where the sentences begin: ☺

Text 2: Fold the sheet along the dotted lines. Draw ☺ at the beginning of each sentence. Check your work.

Text 3: Fold the sheet again along the dotted lines. Find the sentences. Put in the capital letters with a coloured pencil at the beginning of each sentence. Check your work.

1

☺ Dad is at the fish shop. ☺ The fish is fresh.
☺ The fish is on a dish. ☺ Bob can smell the fish.
☺ Bob gets the fish. ☺ He runs to the cat flap.

2

Dad is at the fish shop. The fish is fresh. The fish is on a dish. Bob can smell the fish. Bob gets the fish. He runs to the cat flap.

3

dad is at the fish shop. the fish is fresh. the fish is on a dish. bob can smell the fish. bob gets the fish. he runs to the cat flap.

Did you spot 6 missing capitals letters?

This exercise is to allow the learners to see the sentence as a unit of meaning. They will need a lot of help with this task initially. Self-correcting their own work will help them understand the task. This sheet may be photocopied by the purchaser. © Phonic Books Ltd 2013.

Lesson 13 – Unit 13

Dictation

Words with the following letter pattern:

th

Read each sentence twice before the learner writes it down. If necessary, write the high-frequency words with complex spellings on a board for the learner to refer to.

Beth went **to** Alf's shop.
"**I** can **have a** bit **of** this and **a** bit **of** that,"
thinks Beth.
Frank and Beth drank hot broth.
Tam and Sam get **the** thin rug.
"**I** will get **a** thin rod and fix it," thinks Dad.

High-frequency words with complex spellings in the above text are:

to, I, have, a, of, the

Lesson 13 - Unit 13: th

Reading and spelling words with <th>

this	✓	___ ___ ___
thing		___ ___ ___
moth		___ ___ ___
that		___ ___ ___
think		___ ___ ___
maths		___ ___ ___
froth		___ ___ ___
them		___ ___ ___
path		___ ___ ___

Teaching aims: Reading and spelling words with the <th> spelling

Teaching guidelines: Fold this sheet along the dotted line. Ask the pupil to read the words on the left and tick the words she/he has read correctly. Ask the pupil to turn over the sheet and dictate the words to the pupil. Ask the pupil to spell the words by segmenting and sounding out the sounds as she/he writes them on the lines. Ask the pupil to open the sheet and tick the words she/he has spelled correctly.

Reading and spelling

Beth runs to Alf's shop.

She asks for a bit of this.

Then she asks for a bit of that.

__ __ __ __   __ __ __ __ to __ __ __'__

__ __ __ __.

She __ __ __ __ __ for a __ __ __ of

__ __ __ __.

__ __ __ __ she __ __ __ __ for a

__ __ __ of __ __ __ __.

Copy the text in the top scroll to the bottom scroll. Write a sound on each line e.g.: th a t
This activity can also be used for dictation. Fold the sheet over. The pupil can self-correct
his/her own dictation. This sheet may be photocopied by the purchaser. © Phonic Books Ltd
2013.

Punctuation - sentences with capital letters and full stops.

Tasks: Text 1: Read the text and note where the sentences begin: ☺ and end●

Text 2: Fold the sheet along the dotted lines. Draw ☺ at the beginning of each sentence and put in the full stop ● Check your work.

Text 3: Fold the sheet again along the dotted lines. Find the sentences. Put in the capital letters with a coloured pencil at the beginning of each sentence and the full stops● at the end of the sentence. Check your work.

1

☺ Dad sits at his desk● ☺ Dad will fix his ship with a thin rod● ☺ Sam and Tam rush in with Tim and Josh● ☺ Then the ship tilts● ☺ Dad is cross●

2

Dad sits at his desk   Dad will fix his ship with a thin rod   Sam and Tam rush in with Tim and Josh Then the ship tilts   Dad is cross

---

3

dad sits at his desk   dad will fix his ship with a thin rod   sam and Tam rush in with Tim and Josh then the ship tilts   dad is cross

Did you spot: 5 missing capital letters?
5 missing full stops?

This exercise is to allow the learners to see the sentence as a unit of meaning. They will need a lot of help with this task initially. Self-correcting their own work will help them understand the task. This sheet may be purchased by the purchaser. © Phonic Books Ltd 2013.

Lesson 14 – Unit 14

Dictation

Words with the following letter pattern:

ck

Read each sentence twice before the learner writes it down. If necessary, write the high-frequency words with complex spellings on a board for the learner to refer to.

Raj picks up **his** back pack **to** get **a** red pen.
Mum gets **a** shock and thinks Raj **is** ill.
Raj **has** red spots on **his** neck.
"Shall **I** pick **the** black socks?" asks Jim.
Mum checks that Viv **has a** snack.

High-frequency words with complex spellings in the above text are:

his, to, a, is, has, his, I, the

Lesson 14 - Unit 14: ck

Reading and spelling words with <ck>

duck	✓	__ __ ___
pick		__ __ __
trick		__ __ __ __
black		__ __ __
peck		__ __ ___
socks		__ __ __ __
speck		__ __ __ __
stick		__ __ ___
truck		__ __ ___

Teaching aims: Reading and spelling words with the <ck> spelling

Teaching guidelines: Fold this sheet along the dotted line. Ask the pupil to read the words on the left and tick the words she/he has read correctly. Ask the pupil to turn over the sheet and dictate the words to the pupil. Ask the pupil to spell the words by segmenting and sounding out the sounds as she/he writes them on the lines. Ask the pupil to open the sheet and tick the words she/he has spelled correctly.

Reading and spelling

Jim went to the sock shop.

He got a black sock and a thick sock.

He left with lots of socks.

___ ___ ___   ___ ___ ___ ___   to the   ___ ___ ___

___ ___ ___.

He ___ ___ ___   a ___ ___ ___ ___   ___ ___ ___

___ ___ ___   a ___ ___ ___ ___   ___ ___ ___.

He ___ ___ ___ ___   ___ ___ ___

___ ___ ___ ___   of ___ ___ ___ ___.

Copy the text in the top scroll to the bottom scroll. Write a sound on each line e.g.: <u>s</u> <u>o</u> <u>ck</u>
This activity can also be used for dictation. Fold the sheet over. The pupil can self-correct
his/her own dictation. This sheet may be photocopied by the purchaser. © Phonic Books Ltd.
2013.

Punctuation - sentences with capital letters and full stops.

Tasks: Text 1: Read the text and note where the sentences begin: ☺ and end●

Text 2: Fold the sheet along the dotted lines. Draw ☺ at the beginning of each sentence and put in the full stop ● Check your work.

Text 3: Fold the sheet again along the dotted lines. Find the sentences. Put in the capital letters with a coloured pencil at the beginning of each sentence and the full stops● at the end of the sentence. Check your work.

1

☺ Viv packs for the trip● ☺ Mum helps Viv pack●

☺ Viv ticks a vest and thick socks on her list●

☺ Mum packs a snack● ☺ Viv gets the bus●

2

Viv packs for the trip   Mum helps Viv pack
Viv ticks a vest and thick socks on her list
Mum packs a snack   Viv gets the bus

3

viv packs for the trip   mum helps Viv pack
viv ticks a vest and thick socks on her list
mum packs a snack   viv gets the bus

Did you spot: 5 missing capital letters?
5 missing full stops?

This exercise is to allow the learners to see the sentence as a unit of meaning. They will need a lot of help with this task initially. Self-correcting their own work will help them understand the task. This sheet may be photocopied by the purchaser. © Phonic Books Ltd 2013.

Lesson 15 – Unit 15

Dictation

Words with the following letter pattern:

ng

Read each sentence twice before the learner writes it down. If necessary, write the high-frequency words with complex spellings on a board for the learner to refer to.

Dot ran up **a** long stem and sang **a** song.

A strong wind flung Dot in **to the** pond.

Ken sits on **a** swing **to** think.

It **is** spring. Red Bill sings **a** song and flaps **his** wings.

Flop picks up **the** ring and flings it in **to** the pond.

Common words with complex spellings in the above text are:

a, to, the, is, his

Lesson 15 - Unit 15: ng

Reading and spelling words with <ng>

ring	✓	___ ___ ___	
song		___ ___ ___	
bring		___ ___ ___ ___	
fling		___ ___ ___ ___	
hang		___ ___ ___	
long		___ ___ ___	
sting		___ ___ ___ ___	
cling		___ ___ ___	
rang		___ ___ ___	

Teaching aims: Reading and spelling words with the <ng> spelling

Teaching guidelines: Fold this sheet along the dotted line. Ask the pupil to read the words on the left and tick the words she/he has read correctly. Ask the pupil to turn over the sheet and dictate the words to the pupil. Ask the pupil to spell the words by segmenting and sounding out the sounds as she/he writes them on the lines. Ask the pupil to open the sheet and tick the words she/he has spelled correctly.

Reading and spelling

It is spring.

Red Bill sings a song and flaps his wings.

Red Bill sings at the top of his lungs.

__ __ is __ __ __ __ __.

__ __ __ __ __ __ __ __ __

a __ __ __ __ __ __ __ __ __ __ __

his __ __ __ __.

__ __ __ __ __ __ __ __ __ __ at

the __ __ __ of his __ __ __ __.

Copy the text in the top scroll to the bottom scroll. Write a sound on each line e.g.: s i ng s
This activity can also be used for dictation. Fold the sheet over. The pupil can self-correct
his/her own dictation.   This sheet may be photocopied by the purchaser. © Phonic Books Ltd
2013.

Punctuation - sentences with capital letters and full stops.

Tasks: Text 1: Read the text and note where the sentences begin: ☺ and end●

Text 2: Fold the sheet along the dotted lines. Draw ☺ at the beginning of each sentence and put in the full stop● Check your work.

Text 3: Fold the sheet again along the dotted lines. Find the sentences. Put in the capital letters with a coloured pencil at the beginning of each sentence and the full stops● at the end of the sentence. Check your work.

1

☺Dot ran up a stem● ☺Then Dot felt a strong wind● ☺She hung on to the stem● ☺The wind sent Dot into the pond ● ☺Pip flung a string to Dot●

2

Dot ran up a stem Then Dot felt a strong wind She hung on to the stem The wind sent Dot into the pond Pip flung a string to Dot

---

3

dot ran up a stem   then Dot felt a strong wind she hung on to the stem the wind sent Dot into the pond   pip flung a string to Dot

Did you spot: 5 missing capital letters?
5 missing full stops?

This exercise is to allow the learners to see the sentence as a unit of meaning. They will need a lot of help with this task initially. Self-correcting their own work will help them understand the task. This sheet may be photocopied by the purchaser. © Phonic Books Ltd 2013.

Lesson 16 – Unit 16

Dictation

Words with the following letter pattern:

qu -ve

Read each sentence twice before the learner writes it down. If necessary, write the high-frequency words with complex spellings on a board for the learner to refer to.

Pip and Tess have to **go** on **a** quest **to** get **the** lost chest.

"Pip, let us quit this quest," **says** Tess.

Tess gives rings **to the** big squid that lives on **the** rocks.

"Quick, Quin, get **into the** bed," **said** Chen.

"I will not have **a** dog in **a** bed," **said** Mum.

Common words with complex spellings in the above text are:

go, a, to, the, says, into, said

68

Lesson 16 - Unit 16: qu

Reading and spelling words with <qu>

quit	✓	____ __ __ __
quick		____ __ __ __
quack		____ __ __ __
quilt		____ __ __ __ __
quill		____ __ __ __
quest		____ __ __ __ __
quiz		____ __ __
squid		____ __ __ __
quench		____ __ __ __ __ __

Teaching aims: Reading and spelling words with the <qu> spelling

Teaching guidelines: Fold this sheet along the dotted line. Ask the pupil to read the words on the left and tick the words she/he has read correctly. Ask the pupil to turn over the sheet and dictate the words to the pupil. Ask the pupil to spell the words by segmenting and sounding out the sounds as she/he writes them on the lines. Ask the pupil to open the sheet and tick the words she/he has spelled correctly.

This sheet may be photocopied by the purchaser. © Phonic Books Ltd 2013.

Lesson 16 - Unit 16: ve

Reading and spelling words with <ve>

live	✓	__ __ __	
give		__ __	
have		__ __	
lives		__ __ __ __	
gives		__ __ __ __	
delve		__ __ __	
elves		__ __ __ __	
shelves		__ __ __ __ __	

Teaching aims: Reading and spelling words with the <ve> spelling

Teaching guidelines: Fold this sheet along the dotted line. Ask the pupil to read the words on the left and tick the words she/he has read correctly. Ask the pupil to turn over the sheet and dictate the words to the pupil. Ask the pupil to spell the words by segmenting and sounding out the sounds as she/he writes them on the lines. Ask the pupil to open the sheet and tick the words she/he has spelled correctly.

Reading and spelling

Pip and Tess go on a quest.

Tess is fed up and asks to quit.

Pip is quick to say, "No, it is a quest. We

must go on."

___ ___ ___ ___ ___ ___ ___ ___ ___ **go**

___ ___ a ___ ___ ___ ___.

___ ___ ___ is ___ ___ ___ ___ ___.

___ ___ ___ ___ ___ ___ to ___ ___ ___.

___ ___ ___ is ___ ___ ___ to say, "No,

___ ___ is a ___ ___ ___ ___. We

___ ___ ___ ___ go ___ ___."

Copy the text in the top scroll to the bottom scroll. Write a sound on each line e.g.: <u>qu</u> <u>e</u> <u>s</u> <u>t</u>
This activity can also be used for dictation. Fold the sheet over. The pupil can self-correct
his/her own dictation. This sheet may be photocopied by the purchaser. © Phonic Books Ltd
2013.

Punctuation - sentences with capital letters and full stops.

Tasks: Text 1: Read the text and note where the sentences begin: ☺ and end ●

Text 2: Fold the sheet along the dotted lines. Draw ☺ at the beginning of each sentence and put in the full stop● Check your work.

Text 3: Fold the sheet again along the dotted lines. Find the sentences. Put in the capital letters with a coloured pencil at the beginning of each sentence and the full stops● at the end of the sentence. Check your work.

1

☺Pup Quin is in Chen's bed● ☺Mum tells Quin to get off the bed● ☺Chen asks Nan to fix Quin a quilt● ☺Quin loves his quilt● ☺He is snug in his bed●

2

Pup Quin is in Chen's bed   Mum tells Quin to get off the bed   Chen asks Nan to fix Quin a quilt Quin loves his quilt   He is snug in his bed

----

3

pup Quin is in Chen's bed   mum tells Quin to get off the bed   chen asks Nan to fix Quin a quilt quin loves his quilt   he is snug in his bed

Did you spot: 5 missing capital letters?
                      5 missing full stops?

This exercise is to allow the learners to see the sentence as a unit of meaning. They will need a lot of help with this task initially. Self-correcting their own work will help them understand the task. This sheet may be photocopied by the purchaser. © Phonic Books 2013.

Lesson 17 – Unit 17

Dictation

Words with the following letter patterns:

wh – and two-syllable words

Read each sentence twice before the learner writes it down. If necessary, write the high-frequency words with complex spellings on a board for the learner to refer to.

When Meg **was a** pup, **a** bad man left Meg on **a** path.

Meg **was** sad and upset. "Which path shall **I** run on?"

Meg ran along **a** plank and fell **into the** pond.

When Dan got back with Meg, **his** Dad **said**, "**You** cannot have **a** dog. Bob, **the** cat, will get upset."

Common words with complex spellings in the above text are:

was, a, I, into, the, his, said, you

74

Lesson 17 - Unit 17: wh

Reading and spelling words with <wh>

when	✓
which	
whack	
whip	
whizz	
whiff	
whim	
whelk	
whisk	

Teaching aims: Reading and spelling words with the <wh> spelling

Teaching guidelines: Fold this sheet along the dotted line. Ask the pupil to read the words on the left and tick the words she/he has read correctly. Ask the pupil to turn over the sheet and dictate the words to the pupil. Ask the pupil to spell the words by segmenting and sounding out the sounds as she/he writes them on the lines. Ask the pupil to open the sheet and tick the words she/he has spelled correctly.

Lesson 17 - Unit 17

Reading and spelling words with two syllables

sunset	✓	__ __ __ __ __ __	
picnic		__ __ __ __ __ __	
cannot		__ __ __ __ __ __	
bedbug		__ __ __ __ __ __	
rabbit		__ __ __ __ __ __	
kidnap		__ __ __ __ __ __	
invent		__ __ __ __ __ __	
upset		__ __ __ __ __	
magnet		__ __ __ __ __ __	

Teaching aims: Reading and spelling words with the two syllables

Teaching guidelines: Fold this sheet along the dotted line. Ask the pupil to read the words on the left and tick the words she/he has read correctly. Ask the pupil to turn over the sheet and dictate the words to the pupil. Ask the pupil to spell the words by segmenting and sounding out the sounds as she/he writes them on the lines. Ask the pupil to open the sheet and tick the words she/he has spelled correctly.

Reading and spelling

When Meg bit Dad's jacket, Dad had to punish Meg.

He put Meg in the shed.

Meg was upset.

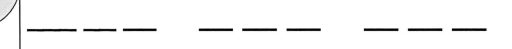

___ ___ ___   ___ ___ ___   ___ ___ ___

___ ___ ___ ' ___   ___ ___ ___ ___ ___ ___ ___,

___ ___ ___   ___ ___ ___   to   ___ ___ ___ ___ ___ ___

___ ___ ___.

He put ___ ___ ___   ___ ___ the ___ ___ ___.

___ ___ ___ was ___ ___ ___ ___ ___ ___.

Copy the text in the top scroll to the bottom scroll. Write a sound on each line e.g.: wh i ch
This activity can also be used for dictation. Fold the sheet over. The pupil can self-correct
his/her own dictation. This sheet may be photocopied by the purchaser. © Phonic Books Ltd
2013.

Punctuation - sentences with capital letters and full stops

Task: Read the text and note where the sentences begin and end.
Put in the capital letters and full stops.

a bad man left Meg, the pup, on a path meg was sad and upset meg ran onto a plank she fell into a pond she got wet meg swam to the bank just then Dan went past meg ran to him dan went home with Meg meg still lives with Dan

Did you spot:
10 missing capital letters?
10 missing full stops?

This exercise is to allow the learners to see the sentence as a unit of meaning. They will need a lot of help with this task initially. Self-correcting their own work will help them understand the task. This sheet may be photocopied by the purchaser. © Phonic Books 2013.

Lesson 18 – Unit 18

Dictation

Words with the following letter pattern:

Past tense of verbs with -ed

Read each sentence twice before the learner writes it down. If necessary, write the high-frequency words with complex spellings on a board for the learner to refer to.

> Sam patted Tam on **the** back.
> Tam sat up, blinked and got up.
> Tam tripped and slipped on **the** steps.
> **The** chimps munched and crunched and snacked.
> Meg sniffed **the** vest and then jumped and yelped at **the** chest.
> Liz lifted **the** lid and Dan jumped up.

High-frequency word with complex spelling in the above text is: the

Lesson 18 Unit 18: -ed

Reading and spelling verbs with past tense <-ed>

patted	✓
blinked	
tripped	
chatted	
dragged	
licked	
mended	
dropped	
rubbed	

Teaching aims: Reading and spelling words with past tense -ed

Teaching guidelines: Fold this sheet along the dotted line. Ask the pupil to read the words on the left and tick the words she/he has read correctly. Ask the pupil to turn over the sheet and dictate the words to the pupil. Ask the pupil to spell the words by segmenting and sounding out the sounds as she/he writes them on the lines. Ask the pupil to open the sheet and tick the words she/he has spelled correctly.

Reading and spelling

The clock rang.

Sam jumped up.

Tam blinked and got up.

Sam and Tam crept past Josh.

The __ __ __ __ __ __ __ __.

__ __ __ __ __ __ __ __ __ up.

__ __ __ __ __ __ __ __ __ __ __

__ __ __ __ __ __ __ __ __.

__ __ __ __ __ __ __ __ __

__ __ __ __ __

__ __ __ __ __ __ __ __ __.

Copy the text in the top scroll to the bottom scroll. Write a sound on each line e.g.: j u m p ed
This activity can also be used for dictation. Fold the sheet over. The pupil can self-correct
his/her own dictation. This sheet may be photocopied by the purchaser. © Phonic Books Ltd
2013.

Punctuation - sentences with capital letters and full stops

Task: Read the text and note where the sentences begin and end.
         Put in the capital letters and full stops.

dan ran up the steps he jumped into an
old chest dan's leg hit the lid of the chest
it slammed shut raj and Liz hunted for
Dan meg led the kids to the old chest liz
lifted the lid of the chest dan jumped up

Did you spot:
9 missing capital letters?
9 missing full stops?

This exercise is to allow the learners to see the sentence as a unit of meaning. They will need a lot of help with this task initially. Self-correcting their own work will help them understand the task. This sheet may be photocopied by the purchaser. © Phonic Books Ltd 2013.

Lesson 19 – Unit 19

Dictation

Word ending <-ing> in two-syllable words

Read each sentence twice before the learner writes it down. If necessary, write the high-frequency words with complex spellings on a board for the learner to refer to.

Liz **is** sticking **to the** path.
Chen **is** standing on **the** quicksand.
Raj **is** helping Chen.
Liz **is holding a** branch **so** that Chen and Raj can get **hold of** it.
Dan **is** clasping **the** elf dust and **is** wishing that **he** can **be as** big **as** a frog.

High-frequency words with complex spellings in the above text are:

is, to, the, is, holding, a, so, hold, of, he, be, as

84

Lesson 19 - Unit 19: -ing

Reading and spelling verbs with <-ing>

Word	✓	Spelling
patting	✓	— — — — — —
swimming		— — — — — —
tripping		— — — — — —
chatting		— — — — —
dragging		— — — — — —
licking		— — — — —
mending		— — — — —
dropping		— — — — — —
rubbing		— — — — —

Teaching aims: Reading and spelling verbs with past participle -ing

Teaching guidelines: Fold this sheet along the dotted line. Ask the pupil to read the words on the left and tick the words she/he has read correctly. Ask the pupil to turn over the sheet and dictate the words to the pupil. Ask the pupil to spell the words by segmenting and sounding out the sounds as she/he writes them on the lines. Ask the pupil to open the sheet and tick the words she/he has spelled correctly.

Reading and spelling

Chen is sinking in the quicksand.

Liz holds a branch for Chen to grab hold of.

Then Chen, Raj and Liz picnic, sitting on the grass.

___ __ __ is __ __ __ __ __ __

__ __ the __ __ __ __ __ __ __ .

__ __ __ holds a __ __ __ __ __ for

__ __ __ to __ __ __ __ hold of.

___ __ __ __ __ __ __, __ __ __

and ___ __ __ __ __ __ __ __ __

__ __ __ __ __ __ on the grass.

Copy the text in the top scroll to the bottom scroll. Write a sound on each line e.g.: s i tt i ng
This activity can also be used for dictation. Fold the sheet over. The pupil can self-correct
his/her own dictation.   This sheet may be photocopied by the purchaser. © Phonic Books Ltd
2013.

Punctuation - sentences with capital letters and full stops

<u>Task:</u>   Read the text and note where the sentences begin and end.
Put in the capital letters and full stops.

wilf and Dan went on a fishing trip wilf had a fishing rod and a can with grubs in it wilf began to nod off a bag of elf dust fell from his pocket dan held some elf dust wishing he was as big as a frog dan began to shrink

Did you spot:
6 missing capital letters?
6 missing full stops?

This exercise is to allow the learners to see the sentence as a unit of meaning. They will need a lot of help with this task initially. Self-correcting their own work will help them understand the task. This sheet may be photocopied by the purchaser. © Phonic Books 2013.

Lesson 20 - Unit 20

Dictation

Words with the following letter pattern:

Word ending <-le> in two-syllable words

Read each sentence twice before the learner writes it down. If necessary, write the high-frequency words with complex spellings on a board for the learner to refer to.

Sam and Josh **have** apples and **a** bottle **of** pop.

Sam will not **give** Josh **the** paddle.

Josh stumbles **into the** pond.

Sam can **see** lots **of** bubbles in **the** pond.

Then Josh jumps up in **the** middle **of the** pond.

Sam **gives** Josh **a** cuddle.

Common words with complex spellings in the above text are:

have, a, of, give, the, into, see, gives

Lesson 20 - Unit 20: -le

Reading and spelling with <-le>

paddle	✓	_ _ _ _
thimble		_ _ _ _ _
gobble		_ _ _ _
puddle		_ _ _ _
pebble		_ _ _ _
little		_ _ _
crumble		_ _ _ _ _
apple		_ _ _
grumble		_ _ _ _ _

Teaching aims: Reading and spelling verbs with past participle -ing

Teaching guidelines: Fold this sheet along the dotted line. Ask the pupil to read the words on the left and tick the words she/he has read correctly. Ask the pupil to turn over the sheet and dictate the words to the pupil. Ask the pupil to spell the words by segmenting and sounding out the sounds as she/he writes them on the lines. Ask the pupil to open the sheet and tick the words she/he has spelled correctly.

Reading and spelling

Pip and Tess smelt the apple crumble.

Pip nibbled the crumble.

Pip wobbled and fell into the dish.

_ _ _ _   _ _ _   _ _ _ _

_ _ _ _ _   the   _ _ _

_ _ _ _ _ _ _ .

_ _ _   _ _ _ _ _   the

_ _ _ _ _ _ .

_ _ _   _ _ _ _ _   and

_ _ _   into the   _ _ _ .

Copy the text in the top scroll to the bottom scroll. Write a sound on each line e.g.: <u>a</u> <u>pp</u> <u>le</u>
This activity can also be used for dictation. Fold the sheet over. The pupil can self-correct
his/her own dictation.   This sheet may be photocopied by the purchaser. © Phonic Books Ltd
2013.

Punctuation - entences with capital letters and full stops

Task: Read the text and note where the sentences begin and end.
        Put in the capital letters and full stops.

sam and Josh have a picnic in the pond
josh asks Sam for the paddle sam tells
Josh he is too little josh grabs the paddle
from Sam josh tumbles into the pond
sam cannot see Josh josh jumps up sam
gives Josh the paddle

Did you spot:
8 missing capital letters?
8 missing full stops?

This exercise is to allow the learners to see the sentence as a unit of meaning. They will need a lot of help with this task initially. Self-correcting their own work will help them understand the task. This sheet may be photocopied by the purchaser. © Phonic Books Ltd 2013.